THE
LORD'S PRAYER:
WALK IN LOVE

Blessings

By Cynthia Davis

Cynthia Davis

Davis, Cynthia.
    Lord's Prayer: Walk in Love / Cynthia Davis.

ISBN: 978-0-9844723-4-5

1. Lord's Prayer—Non-Fiction. 2. Way of Love—Non-Fiction. 3. Episcopal Church—Non Fiction 4. Devotional—Non Fiction. 6. Religious study—Non Fiction. I. Title.

The Lord's Prayer: Walk in Love

WITH THANKS

To my husband Ken for years of loving support.

To Linda White and Elaine Wilson for all their encouragement, and editing of my ideas.

To my friends who didn't let me give up.

To all those who shared their enthusiasm for the project.

To all who have supported my writing over the years.

To each reader and fellow pilgrim on the way.

May you be blessed.

TABLE OF CONTENTS

WELCOME

A basic part of all Christian life is the Lord's Prayer. We recite it at nearly every worship service. Many of us learned it as children and return to it whenever we need comfort. Hospital and hospice chaplains report that women and men deep in the grip of dementia, Alzheimer's, or on the verge of death can still respond and even recite the familiar words.

Come on a journey with me that will inspire you, as we look at the words of this prayer in a new way. We will see how it is a life changing and life empowering prayer that calls us to be part of God's love for all, so that we can *walk in love, just as Christ loved us and gave himself for us a fragrant offering and sacrifice to God* (Ephesians 5:2).

The Lord's Prayer is what we pray. We will explore how the Lord's Prayer encapsulates the *Way of Love* practices as outlined by The Most Reverend Michael Curry, Presiding Bishop of the Episcopal Church, while offering a framework for how to live God's love in our day-to-day lives.

In our study we will look at the familiar wording of the Lord's Prayer and get inspiration from some alternate translations and versions. Sometimes hearing the words from a different source can help us gain new insight into the meaning, implications, and inspiration available.

Each chapter will offer the chance to look at scripture and ways to apply the prayer and scripture to our faith journey. In the tradition of the Episcopal *Book of Common Prayer*, we will collect the thoughts together at the end of each chapter in a prayer.

The Lord's Prayer: Walk in Love

By studying the words of the prayer, with references to scripture and other resources, you will gain new insight into the Lord's Prayer and into living as a member of God's Kingdom. Questions at the end of each chapter reinforce the study, while a closing prayer exercise opens the heart and mind to God's work in our lives.

In this book,

- We Prayerfully study the Lord's Prayer line by line.
- We See the *Way of Love* in the Lord's Prayer.
- We Read scripture to deepen our understanding of the Lord's Prayer.
- We Apply the Lord's Prayer in our life with thought-provoking questions.
- We Pause to connect with God.

Writing this book has amazed me with new ways of looking at the familiar words, and I hope it will do the same for you. As is often the case, the author is only what someone once called a "scribe for the eternal." The words that spill onto the pages of books often come from someplace beyond our conscious minds and enter the heart of both writer and reader. I pray that you will be blessed by this book.

In Christ,

Cynthia Davis

OUR FATHER IN HEAVEN, HOLY IS YOUR NAME

The first line of this very familiar prayer takes us directly to the foot of the throne of God. We are reminded that our relationship to God is both intimate and intimidating. N.T. Wright, Anglican Bishop of Durham, England, notes that **this prayer is "part of the holy boldness, the almost cheeky celebration of the sheer grace and goodness of the living God."**[1]

The prayer begins as we address "Our Father." These words immediately conjure up images of family relationship. In the Aramaic, it is *Abba,* a form of Daddy. To call the Holy One of Israel by such an intimate and friendly title was probably shocking to the first disciples. God is "high and lifted up," not addressable as Papa. Yet, our Lord taught the disciples, and us, to say "Hello Daddy" as we begin this prayer.

We could just as easily say our mother and feel the same relationship to those who first cared for us. Some alternative translations say, "Breath of life" or "Breath, the Light of all" (a supposedly more precise translation from the Syrian/Aramaic). That calls us perhaps to an even more intimate understanding and recalls how "the Lord God breathed into the nostrils…" (Genesis 1).

The New Zealand Prayer Book expands the salutation to be, "Eternal Spirit, Earth-maker, Pain-bearer, Life-giver, Source of all that is and that shall be, Father and Mother of us all, Loving God." Praying these words gives us an awe-inspiring glimpse at the many attributes of God, all of which nurture and enfold us.

---

[1] NT Wright, *The Lord and His Prayer*, (William B. Eerdmans Publishing Co. 1996) pg. 13

After being reminded that God is intimately connected to us, as parent, as life-giving breath, and as source, we are reminded that God is infinitely distant. In fact, God is "in heaven." Jesus wants us to remember that the One who created us is greater than the earthly parents who birthed and nurtured us.

Where exactly is heaven? Of course, to the ancient peoples, heaven was the arch above us. As modern inhabitants of the earth, and inheritors of space travel, we know that heaven and the universe is much more than our ancestors could have imagined. It seems to be infinitely distant and, we are told, ever expanding. Yet, our God is as close as a loving parent.

The New Zealand Prayer Book opens this up more broadly by stating that God "in whom is heaven" is the one we are addressing. God is our "Eternal Spirit, Earth-maker, Pain-bearer, Life-giver, Source of all that is and that shall be, Father and Mother of us all, Loving God" and God also encompasses heaven itself. God is throughout and beyond the known universe. And God is intimately relating to each of us as Father, Mother, Source, Breath, Life-giver! God created and inhabits the realm of space, which is beyond comprehension. Even more amazing, **God lives within each of us just as fully. Heaven is within, as well as beyond us.**

In this we are reminded that God is infinitely Holy. The traditional version of the Lord's Prayer says, "Hallowed by thy name." Hallowed means consecrated, revered, honored. It comes from the Old English words *hālgian* and *hālga*, which can be translated as holy. Newer translations say, "Holy is your name." The root of the word holy is from the Old English word *hālig*, which has the connotation of being whole. The prayer makes us aware that God is to be revered and that God is all wholeness.

In reciting "Our Father, who art in heaven," we are called to acknowledge from the start that God, while intimately connected to us from the very beginning, is in fact, far beyond us. *The New Zealand Prayer Book* again speaks this beautifully, "The hallowing of your name echo through the universe!"

The mystery of God's immense love is summed up in these first few words of the prayer. **We are invited into relationship with the holy One who is the Source of all, and who loves us like a parent.**

WE SEE THE *WAY OF LOVE* IN THE LORD'S PRAYER

The *Way of Love* practices, outlined by Episcopal Presiding Bishop Michael Curry, call us to pray. To pray, according to the *Way of Love* is to pause and listen to and for God.

> "[Pray is to] dwell intentionally with God each day…to come before God with humble hearts, boldly offering our thanksgivings and concerns to God or simply listening for God's voice in our lives and in the world. Whether in thought, word or deed, individually or corporately, when we pray, we invite and dwell in God's loving presence."[2]

The opening words of the Lord's Prayer invite us to come to God as our loving Abba (or Amma). We acknowledge that God is truly Holy and beyond our comprehension. Even so, God is intimately involved in "our lives and in the world," as *Way of Love* states. In the Lord's Prayer, we are affirming God's intimate relationship to us. We are connected to the Holy, with God who is in and yet is beyond all creation.

---

[2] https://www.episcopalchurch.org/way-of-love/practice/pray

14

The Lord's Prayer: Walk in Love

We know that God will hear our "thanksgivings and concerns" no matter how we approach God. The *Way of Love* notes, "when we pray, we invite and dwell in God's loving presence." The Lord's Prayer; in the very first phrases, calls us into God's presence as beloved children. **We can come and sit on our Abba's lap and tell God what is on our minds!**

Some of the richest memories of my childhood are cuddling into my father's lap at bedtime for a story. Sometimes it was also a time to share the events of the day with my parents. It was the perfect way to end each day. We can have that same comfort in our heavenly Father's embrace as we recognize God as Abba/Amma—the One who loves us totally. We can sit in our Father's lap and tell God what's going on in our lives. God loves for us to come, sit with God, and let God be part of the fabric of our daily lives. The Lord's Prayer gives us one way of doing that.

WE READ SCRIPTURE

The Lord's Prayer originates when the disciples ask Jesus "teach us to pray as the rabbis teach their disciples." The scene is found in Luke 11:1-4 and in Matthew 6:9-15. In the Luke version of the story, Jesus goes on to explain that God does listen to our requests. God is more than just a friend who we might ask for bread. That friend might at first refuse, saying, *Do not bother me; the door has already been locked, and my children are with me in bed; I cannot get up and give you anything.* However, if, like the neighbor, we are persistent, the friend *will get up and give him whatever he needs* (Luke 11:5-8).

Jesus invites his disciples, and us, to continually *Ask, and it will be given to you; search, and you will find; knock, and the door will be opened for you. For everyone who asks receives, and everyone who searches finds, and for everyone who knocks, the door will be opened* (Luke 11:9-10).

In the Matthew version of the Lord's Prayer Jesus concludes his exhortations with encouragement for life.

Do not worry about your life, what you will eat or what you will drink, or about your body, what you will wear...look at the birds of the air; they neither sow nor reap nor gather into barns, and yet your heavenly Father feeds them...Consider the lilies of the field...even Solomon in all his glory was not clothed like one of these. But if God so clothes the grass of the field, which is alive today and tomorrow is thrown into the oven, will he not much more clothe you—you of little faith...your heavenly Father knows that you need all these things. But strive first for the kingdom of God and his righteousness, and all these things will be given to you as well (Matthew 6:25-33).

When sitting in my father's lap, the five-year-old me knew that I could ask for anything. I knew that my earthly father would make every attempt to get whatever it was I wanted. In fact, one year, I asked for a stuffed elephant for Christmas. I'm told they weren't readily available, but somehow, I got my elephant for Christmas. I named her "Mary" and she was my companion for years. My parents had searched and searched until they found what I wanted. Jesus promises that our heavenly Father will do that and so much more.

Jesus teaches the Lord's Prayer as the way to approach God with our requests. The story in both the Gospel of Luke and Gospel of Matthew insist that it is perfectly OK to approach God with our most basic needs, and to address God as our "Abba." **This prayer allows us to come to the Throne of God not as beggars, but as beloved children who can curl up in the lap of a**

16

loving parent. The Lord's Prayer assures us that God wants to hear us and wants to respond

WE APPLY THE LORD'S PRAYER TO OUR LIFE

- ❖ Look at various versions of the Lord's Prayer in the appendix, or online. Pray them each slowly and listen to the words and cadence. Which one speaks to your ear and your heart?
- ❖ "Our Father" or "Abba" is an intimate address for God. Have you ever paused to think about our brashness in praying in that way?
- ❖ *The Way of Love* defines the discipline of pray as to "dwell intentionally with God." How does that coincide with the way you think about prayer?
- ❖ Jesus promises, *Ask, and it will be given to you; search, and you will find; knock, and the door will be opened for you. For everyone who asks receives, and everyone who searches finds, and for everyone who knocks, the door will be opened* (Luke 11:9-10). Can you believe that is true of your prayers?

WE PAUSE TO CONNECT WITH GOD

Use this prayer; or develop your own prayer based on your thoughts from the first line of the Lord's Prayer and this chapter. Offer your heart's desire to God, just as you would if you were sitting on your parent's lap.

Dear Papa/Mama, I cannot believe you love me so much! You are greater than I can understand, and still you care enough for me to listen to my slightest whisper. I know you want me to come to you with my needs, wants, and desires as well as my failures and my fears. Because I trust that you do love me, I lift my heart up to you right now. (Offer any prayers that come to mind). Thank you for loving me. Amen.

18

The Lord's Prayer: Walk in Love

Love - forgive - break boundaries - in small
ways

YOUR KINGDOM COME

Jesus promises that we can, and should, come to God as we would come to a trusted father or mother. We are guaranteed that we are the beloved children of God who wants to give us good things. All we have to do is ask.

The next phrase of the Lord's Prayer asks that God's "Kingdom come." In a world with fewer and fewer monarchies, what might that say to us in the 21st Century? The idea of "kingdom" may conjure up images of knights and princesses and dragons. Or perhaps the Changing of the Guard at Buckingham Palace and royal weddings. Kingdoms are rather far off and distant, and almost fairy-tale like. What kind of kingdom are we asking for?

A kingdom is something special, yet almost archaic in the modern world. An alternative form of the Lord's Prayer from All Saints Fulham, Pryor's Bank, Bishop's Park, London asks that "the Way of your Justice be followed by the people of the world." Perhaps those words help give insight into what we mean when we pray "your Kingdom come." **God's Kingdom is more than just an old-fashioned, romantic way of looking at who is in charge. It is not as much a top-down imposition of power as an indwelling of grace and love that transforms lives.**

This Kingdom is God's leadership (lordship) being shown through each of us. It is the "way of justice followed by the people of the world." It is the People of God becoming the avenue to bless all creation. The coming kingdom is active.

Ellicott's Commentary for English Readers notes that "the prayer had its origin in the Messianic expectations embodied in the picture of the ideal king....Now the kingdom of God...was not, like the kingdoms of the world, one that rested on the despotism of might, but on the acknowledgment of righteousness. It was therefore ever growing to a completeness....Its advance to that completeness might be retarded by man's self-will, and hastened by man's fulfilment of its conditions...therefore we pray that it may 'come' in its fulness, that all created beings may bring their wills into harmony with God's will."[3]

N.T. Wright notes that the Lord's Prayer is, in fact, "the risky, crazy prayer of submission and commission, or, if you like, the prayer of subversion and conversion. It is the way we sign on, in our turn, for the work of the kingdom."[4] **Saying "Your Kingdom come" is about letting go of a "my way or the highway" mentality and saying to God "you are in charge."** It's opening our hearts to enthrone the Holy One, the King of Kings. And it's not easy.

We are conditioned to be individualists by our western culture. Letting someone else, whether monarch or God, be in control, feels like we are giving up our rights. And we are, in fact, giving up the right to claim our own sovereignty. This phrase invites us to become part of building the very Kingdom we pray for. **As we welcome the Kingdom in ourselves, we can bless others so that they, too, may be part of the Kingdom.**

WE SEE THE *WAY OF LOVE* IN THE LORD'S PRAYER

The *Way of Love* practice to bless is a two-way street. We are given God's grace and love in the Kingdom of God. We, in turn, reach out in love to bless one another.

To bless is to "Share faith and unselfishly give and serve...We are empowered by the Spirit to bless everyone we meet,

---

[3] https://www.biblehub.com/commentaries/ellicott/matthew/6.htm
[4] Wright, *The Lord and His Prayer*, pg. 32

22

practicing generosity and compassion, and proclaiming the Good News of God in Christ with hopeful words and selfless actions. We can share our stories of blessing and invite others to the *Way of Love*."[5]

Isn't that exactly what the Kingdom of God is? Isn't it a world where we "unselfishly give and serve, empowered by the Spirit"?

The Kingdom of God is built on the Good News that we are beloved of God. A broken and hurting creation needs, indeed must, hear that message. In telling our Kingdom stories, we bless and invite others into the Kingdom. Our story is, surprisingly, an integral part of God's ongoing story. The Bible story didn't end with the *Book of Revelation*, it continues in each of us. God is making us part of the Kingdom, part of the blessing of creation.

Kingdom making isn't an easy process. It's more like reconstruction. In his book *Mere Christianity*, C.S. Lewis expands the analogy.

He writes, "Imagine yourself as a living house. God comes in to rebuild that house. At first, perhaps, you can understand what He is doing. He is getting the drains right and stopping the leaks in the roof and so on; you knew that those jobs needed doing and so you are not surprised. But presently He starts knocking the house about in a way that hurts abominably and does not seem to make any sense. What on earth is He up to? The explanation is that He is building quite a different house from the one you thought of—throwing out a new wing here, putting on an extra floor there, running up towers, making courtyards. You thought you were being

---

[5] https://www.episcopalchurch.org/way-of-love/practice/bless

renovate my heart

made into a decent little cottage: but He is building a palace. He intends to come and live in it Himself."[6]

Anyone who has ever been part of a home remodel knows it takes longer than planned, every single time! It is not always fun to live in a construction zone. I recall when my husband and I re-did our kitchen, it was weeks and weeks of dust and mess and things not in their place. When God gets to work, as C.S. Lewis says, the renovation is much more extensive than we may anticipate or want. God's work is lifelong.

We may not always enjoy the process. It is really uncomfortable to be under construction. The kitchen remodel involved removing cabinets, ripping up the floor to install new tile. It meant that things weren't in their normal places and that making dinner was more of an adventure than I might have liked. The renovation seemed to stretch on forever. The end result, though, was a lovely new space in which to cook and dine.

The result of God's construction project is that God comes and makes his home with us, builds the Kingdom in us, and with us, and of us. As we become more fully part of that Kingdom, we bless those in our immediate sphere of influence. As the *Way of Love* suggests, we should share our stories of the reconstruction happening in our lives. **When we share how we are being remade into God's Kingdom, and what a blessing it is, others are changed, and they influence still others**. We each become a way to bless others, until someday the Kingdom will come.

---

[6] (Lewis, C.S. (2001). *Mere Christianity*: a revised and amplified edition, with a new introduction, of the three books, Broadcast talks, Christian behavior, and Beyond personality. [San Francisco]: Harper San Francisco. ISBN 0-06-065292-6)

There's an old song that says, "It only takes a spark." When we let God start reconstruction on our lives, we become that spark. It's not a comfy prospect, nor is it a fast fix. God wants to bless us with only the best, and God is a thorough Master Builder. The result will be worth the changes we might think we could live without. When we look back, we will see that we did indeed need the blessing of the renovation of our lives so we can live into and become the Kingdom of God.

WE READ SCRIPTURE

The Kingdom we pray for, and that God desires to build in us, is grounded in grace and love. At the Last Supper Jesus tells his disciples, *If anyone loves Me, he will keep My word; and My Father will love him, and We will come to him and make Our abode with him* (John 14:23).

St. Paul asks the Corinthians, *Do you not know that you are a temple of God and that the Spirit of God dwells in you?* (1 Corinthians 3:16)

That temple, the Kingdom of God, has an eternal foundation and cornerstone. Paul tells the Ephesians *you are...members of the household of God, built upon the foundation of the apostles and prophets, with Christ Jesus himself as the cornerstone. In him the whole structure is joined together and grows into a holy temple in the Lord; in whom you also are built together spiritually into a dwelling-place for God* (Ephesians 2:19-22).

God's blueprint for the reconstruction of our souls makes us into a Temple where God can live. Our current house may be built on unstable and uneven ground. God's new building is on the firm foundation of "Christ as the cornerstone." A cornerstone is the most important part of a building. It's the first one put in place and oriented perfectly so the rest of the building will be square and true.

The same is true of laying tile. When we were redoing the kitchen, we had to be sure the first tile was positioned properly, or the entire floor would have been slightly out of square. By ensuring that the first tile was right, the rest were in the proper orientation. Christ, as our cornerstone and foundation, provides the same true alignment.

One of my favorite hymns uses words from the seventh century which states, "Christ is made the sure foundation/Christ the head and cornerstone/Chosen of the Lord and precious/Binding all the church in one."[7]. **Christ is the cornerstone that aligns each of us into position to be part of the edifice that is the Kingdom of God.**

Because we are such an important part of the Kingdom, we need to make some sort of response to the grace and love that make us part of the Kingdom. That response is encapsulated in Micah 6:8. The prophet says, *He has shown you, O mortal, what is good. And what does the LORD require of you? To act justly and to love mercy and to walk humbly with your God.*

Isaiah 61 gives greater detail about how to live this Kingdom life. The Gospel of Luke tells us that Jesus read this scripture at the synagogue in Nazareth.

The Spirit of the Lord is on me, because he has anointed me to proclaim good news to the poor. He has sent me to proclaim freedom for the prisoners and recovery of sight for the blind,

---

[7] https://hymnary.org/text/christ_is_made_the_sure_foundation Translation by John Mason Neal and music by Henry Purcell

to set the oppressed free, to proclaim the year of the Lord's favor (Luke 4:18-19).

As those being called to bless the world because we are being built into God's Kingdom, we are to "act justly and to love mercy and to walk humbly with your God." We are to proclaim good news, freedom, and ultimately to announce the "Lord's favor." The *Way of* Love says we are to "bless everyone we meet, practicing generosity and compassion, and proclaiming the Good News of God in Christ with hopeful words and selfless actions."

How can we possibly do that? Not in our own strength, but in the power of the Spirit. Chapter 3 of the Letter to the Ephesians ends with a paean of praise and instruction in living into God's Kingdom.

For this reason, I bow my knees before the Father, from whom every family in heaven and on earth takes its name. I pray that, according to the riches of his glory, he may grant that you may be strengthened in your inner being with power through his Spirit, and that Christ may dwell in your hearts through faith, as you are being rooted and grounded in love. I pray that you may have the power to comprehend, with all the saints, what is the breadth and length and height and depth, and to know the love of Christ that surpasses knowledge, so that you may be filled with all the fullness of God. Now to him who by the power at work within us is able to accomplish abundantly far more than all we can ask or imagine, to him be glory in the church and in Christ Jesus to all generations, for ever and ever. Amen (Ephesians 3:14-21).

St. Paul notes that *every family in heaven and on earth* is part of God's Kingdom. Because Christ lives *in your hearts through faith, as you are being rooted and grounded in love* we can *know the love of Christ that surpasses knowledge* and *be filled with the fullness of God.* What a great promise! **The Kingdom is being built of God's love, lived out in each heart.**

Even though we are giving up our own sovereignty in order to allow God's Kingdom to come, we are empowered to be and bring about that Kingdom, and to bless the world. **God re-constructs us purposely to orient us to Christ the cornerstone, so that we can be a temple that blesses others. As God's love changes us, we change the world.**

The Lord's Prayer: Walk in Love

WE APPLY THE LORD'S PRAYER TO OUR LIFE

- ❖ What words or images come to mind as you hear the word "kingdom"? Write down these words and consider how they compare to the Kingdom of God.
- ❖ As members of the Kingdom of God, we are called to make a response in love that will bless others. In your life, how do you bless your part of the world?
- ❖ Construction is hard, messy work. When has God done renovation on your life or heart?
- ❖ Ephesians 2 says we are, *built upon the foundation of the apostles and prophets, with Christ Jesus himself as the cornerstone. In him the whole structure is joined together and grows into a holy temple in the Lord*. How would this citation look if you drew it as a picture?

WE PAUSE TO CONNECT WITH GOD

Write your own prayer; or use this prayer to gather your thoughts about the Kingdom of God. Offer to let yourself be part of the creation of that kingdom of justice, mercy, humility, and love.

Holy God, as we pray "Your Kingdom Come," we realize that you are using us to build your Kingdom. I often feel inadequate and unloving, but You are always busy renovating me. Help me to allow you to work in and through me so that all may obtain freedom and justice in your Kingdom. Amen.

YOUR WILL BE DONE, ON EARTH AS IN HEAVEN

The Lord's Prayer invites us to come to God just as we would to a loving parent. We can curl up in God's arms and tell him what we want, knowing that God will give us what we need when we pray. We know that ultimately and above all, God is Love. Living in relationship to God, we discover that being God's Kingdom is our response, it is the way we bless the world. We are changed, even reconstructed, as we intentionally invite God to live in us.

Our response is to be open and allow God's "will be done, on earth as in heaven." This phrase of the familiar Lord's Prayer should cause us to pause and think about what we are actually promising. We say, "Your will be done!" **We are offering to allow God to be completely and totally in control so that God's will can happen.** What might that mean in our lives?

The New Zealand Prayer Book translation of the Lord's Prayer expands the phrase by saying, "Your heavenly will be done by all created beings! Your commonwealth of peace and freedom sustain our hope and come on earth." A version from Times and Seasons.net similarly asks, "May justice and mercy reign, in our lives and in our world."

God's will for creation is peace, justice, freedom and mercy. As we pray the Lord's Prayer, we are opening ourselves up to be a conduit for God to work through us. We start to learn how to do this from the moment we are baptized.

In the Baptismal covenant of The Episcopal Church, we affirm that we will "proclaim by word and example the Good News of God in Christ, seek and serve Christ in all persons, loving your neighbor as yourself, and strive for justice and peace among all people, and respect the dignity of every human being." Whether these words were said for you as an infant, or you recited them yourself, you have been "marked as Christ's own forever."

We repeat these words every time there is a baptism in church. This helps us learn and internalize what it means to being open to God's will. It is all outlined in the Baptismal words.

We are to make known, "by word and example, the Good News" of God's Love manifested in Jesus Christ.

We are to serve others, recognizing Christ in all people.

We are to love our neighbor, and to love ourselves.

We are to work for justice and peace everywhere, "among all people."

We are to respect the dignity of men, women, and children of all ages, creeds, lifestyles, and colors.

Each of these promises is a manifestation of God's will here among us, now. **Our individual actions are necessary and important in allowing Kingdom work to be done on earth.** As we live and grow in our relationship with God, we learn more and more about what it means to proclaim, serve, love, and work for the justice and peace of God's Kingdom.

The way that you learn and live this self-offering of your life will be different from how I do it. And that is OK. Every one of us is created by God to do our part, large or small, in bringing God's will, God's love, and God's Kingdom to earth.

WE SEE THE *WAY OF LOVE* IN THE LORD'S PRAYER

The *Way of Love* tells us that we learn how to respond with blessing and love as we internalize God's word and call.

In the musical *South Pacific*[8] Lt. Cable sings to Nurse Nellie Forbush that we "have to be taught to hate and fear." The song is a stern reminder that too often we learn the wrong things. We may pick up ungodly messages at home and in school and from associates. In the musical, Nurse Nellie cannot, initially, accept that the man she loves had been married to, and had children with, a South Pacific woman. Lt. Cable is struggling with his own prejudice because he loves a girl on Bali Hai but knows (or thinks he knows) that is wrong because of what he has been "carefully taught."

Children, before they are "taught," know that we are all children of God. Facebook is peppered with memes and pictures of children interacting with one another with no consideration of race, creed, or religion. Perhaps that is why Jesus says, "let the children come for to such belongs the kingdom." (Matthew 19:14) **Children innately believe the best in one another.**

Some adults retain, or reacquire, the ability to look beyond appearances and even actions. Although he experienced some of the worst of human behavior, hatred, and degradation during his imprisonment, Nelson Mandela believed that there was good in everyone. In his autobiography, *Long Walk to Freedom* (1994), he states,

> "I always knew that deep down in every human, there is mercy and generosity. No one is born hating another person because of the color of his skin or his background or his religion. People must learn to hate, and if they can learn to hate, they can be taught to love. For love comes more

[8] https://en.wikipedia.org/wiki/South_Pacific

naturally to the human heart than its opposite. Even in the grimmest times in prison when my comrades and I were pushed to our limits, I would see a glimmer of humanity in one of the guards, perhaps just for a second, but it was enough to reassure me and keep me moving. Man's goodness is a flame that can be hidden but never extinguished."

We imbibe the mistaken messages of hate, fear, prejudice, and anger from our culture and environment. This makes it even more important to seek and learn God's will. Mandela was able to see the "glimmer of humanity" in his guards. We can learn to look for God in one another and celebrate God in them. We can recognize and acknowledge the good rather than reacting to the negatives. **We can be part of the will and Kingdom of God's love on earth.**

The *Way of Love* says we learn "By reading and reflecting on Scripture, especially the life and teachings of Jesus, we draw near to God and God's word dwells in us. When we open our minds and hearts to Scripture, we learn to see God's story and God's activity in everyday life."[9]

When we learn about God's work, we discover that God's will intersects with our life and work. Max Lucado, author and pastor writes, "Your story indwells God's. This is the great promise of the Bible...around us God directs a grander saga, written by his hand, orchestrated by his will, unveiled according to his calendar. And you are a part of it."[10]

God, amazingly, needs us to participate in the grand Story of creation and salvation. Just as we are part of bringing the Kingdom of God to the world, we are necessary to make God's will present in all creation. We are called to speak up against

---

[9] https://www.episcopalchurch.org/way-of-love/practice/learn
[10] https://maxlucado.com/products/gods-story-your-story/

prejudice and injustice. We are empowered to share God's love by respecting and affirming the dignity and rights of every person and all creation. Our service to God through serving one another manifests God's will in the world.

One of the lessons I learned from my parents is a love for living creatures. We always had a dog or two and at least one cat who we treated with respect and love. I think my father probably loved animals more than some people. In fact, he once went a little overboard in his love for God's creatures. There is the family story of how he rescued a family of skunks, when I was only a few months old. To do that, he had to remove the mom and babies from the concrete tank they had fallen into.

Mama Skunk repaid the act of kindness by spraying him. My father regularly teased my mother, saying she didn't "hold her tail down" when he was handing Mama Skunk to her. She invariably responded by insisting the critter had moved her tail. Then she would add that we had to walk on tiptoe all weekend because of the baby skunk hiding under the refrigerator. On Monday, they took the little skunk to the vet for surgery to remove the scent glands, and for a time we had a skunk as a pet.

Whether we serve God's kingdom by caring for the environment and animals, or by standing with those who do not have a voice, or by simply being open and friendly, we are opening the way for God's will to be done. **We are helping to erase the false teachings of the world by helping people learn that God's love is embedded in everything and everyone.** As Mandala said, "Man's goodness is a flame that can be hidden but never extinguished," despite what we may see online and in the nightly news.

36

The Lord's Prayer: Walk in Love

WE READ SCRIPTURE

Jesus helps us learn about God's will through his parables and by the way he lived his life. He warns that *Not everyone that says to me, Lord, Lord, shall enter into the kingdom of heaven; but he that doeth the will of my Father which is in heaven* (Matthew 7:21).

On the other hand, Jesus states *whosoever shall do the will of my Father which is in heaven, the same is my brother, and sister, and mother* (Matthew 12:50). **When we do God's will we live a life that expresses God's love and we are part of Jesus' family!**

Jesus gives us a perfect example of obeying the will of God. As he approached his own death, he struggled with his mortality, pleading for a different way. He prayed desperately, *Father, if You are willing, take this cup from Me. Yet not My will, but Yours be done* (Luke 22:42). Despite his fears, he offers himself fully, *My Father, if this cup cannot pass unless I drink it, may Your will be done* (Matthew 26:42). Jesus bowed to God's way in order that God's will might be done on earth. We, too, are called to be open to God's will in our lives.

In his interactions with the outcasts and sinners of Galilee and Judea, Jesus helps us learn what the will of God is for us. One of the times the Pharisees criticized him for *[welcoming and eating with] sinners* (Luke 15:2b), he responded with the Parable of the Lost Sheep.

Which one of you, having a hundred sheep and losing one of them, does not leave the ninety-nine in the wilderness and go after the one that is lost until he finds it? When he has found it, he lays it on his shoulders and rejoices. And when he comes home, he calls together his friends and neighbors, saying to them, "Rejoice with me, for I have found my sheep that was lost." Just so, I tell you, there will be more joy in heaven over one sinner who repents than over ninety-nine righteous people who need no repentance (Luke 15:4-7).

God's will *is* justice and mercy. God's action *is always* grace. **No one is outside God's love.** Indeed, it may be those who seem to be on the "outside" who are closest to God. It is not up to us to decide who is in or out. As we live into the will of God "on earth as in heaven," we are urged to seek out the ones who feel separate and lost. We are to treasure the disenfranchised, the hurting, and the lost.

Jesus reminds us we can do this because we are intimately linked to God and to the entire family of God. We are invited to *abide in me as I abide in you. Just as the branch cannot bear fruit by itself unless it abides in the vine, neither can you unless you abide in me. I am the vine; you are the branches* (John 15:4-5).

A plant of any kind is only as healthy as the root and main stem. A grape vine has a sturdy trunk, but grapes don't grow on the trunk itself. They grow on the smaller canes that sprout each spring from the branches of the vine. As long as the trunk of the vine is strong and deeply rooted, there will be grapes. We are part of the vine that includes all of creation. **Our task is to align ourselves with the will of God and bear fruit.**

What is that fruit? Jesus says it is to *love one another as I have loved you. No one has greater love than this, to lay down one's life for one's friends. You are my friends if you do what I command you....You did not choose me but I chose you. And I appointed you to go and bear fruit, fruit that will last, so that the Father will give you whatever you ask him in my name* (John 15:12b-16).

God has chosen each of us to be part of the Kingdom and to learn how to bear the fruit we are made to produce. **As we pray "thy will be done, on earth as in heaven" we learn that we are an integral part of bringing that Kingdom to fruition.** We do that by living out God's love to those we meet. God chose us to "go and bear fruit," which we can do because God does abide in us.

WE APPLY THE LORD'S PRAYER TO OUR LIFE

- ❖ The Baptismal covenant says we are to "proclaim by word and example the Good News of God in Christ, seek and serve Christ in all persons, loving your neighbor as yourself, and strive for justice and peace among all people, and respect the dignity of every human being." How do your words and actions help God's will to happen?
- ❖ Learning about God through scripture helps us identify how God is active in our lives. What specific scripture citations inspire you or help you see God's action in your life?
- ❖ Jesus tells the parable of the Good Shepherd to explain that God's will is to find all the lost. In what ways does your life seek those who may be "lost" and unaware of God's love?
- ❖ Each of us is to "bear fruit" as part of the vine that is the Kingdom of God. What is your fruit?

WE PAUSE TO CONNECT WITH GOD

Write your own prayer; or use this prayer to gather your thoughts about how you can help God's will be done "on earth as in heaven."

Loving God, you seek out the one lost sheep, and you call me to do the same. Help me to be a living branch of the vine that is your Kingdom. I want to do your will, although sometimes I find it hard to know exactly what to do. Help me to remember that when I am loving, as you love, then I am doing your will. Amen.

The Lord's Prayer: Walk in Love

GIVE US THIS DAY OUR DAILY BREAD

So far, we have seen that God invites us into prayerful relationship through the words of the Lord's Prayer. This prayer is known by people who perhaps don't know any other prayer; and it can be remembered long after other cognitive prayers have slipped away. **We are invited into a unique child-to-parent relationship as we pray to our Father (Mother, Creator).**

As we pray, we recognize that God's name is Holy. Even as we pray "your kingdom come," we realize that we are part of the blessing involved in making that holy kingdom a reality. We learn that as we pray "your will be done," we are asking God to teach us ways to actively live out our baptismal covenant and work to bring God's will to "earth as in heaven."

The Lord's Prayer continues as we ask that God will "Give us this day our daily bread." *The New Zealand Prayer Book* version uses the phrase, "With the bread we need for today, feed us," while a translation from Syrian Aramaic expands the request to be, "Grant what we need each day in bread and insight."

At first glance this request might almost seem like a demand. In a way it is. We are God's children asking for sustenance. **Just as our own children depend on us for food, we depend on God to provide what we need.** The prayer is an acknowledgement that we must have food to survive. However, we might ask ourselves, "How much do I really need?" Can I simply rest and trust that God will indeed supply what I need? Leslie Leyland Fields wrote her own version of the Lord's Prayer including the line, "we ask, would you give us each day the food we need (but no more, no less, so we live by trust more than food)?"

In a culture that says, "more is better" and advertises that if I "want it now," I can have it, we may find it hard to be satisfied with simple bread and wine. Yet as Omar Khayyam's poem the *Rubaiyat* says, "A loaf of bread, a jug of wine, and thou" are really all we need. We may sometimes forget that we are in a love relationship with God who calls us "beloved." To rest with and in God, can make, as Khayyam states, "Wilderness were Paradise enow."

Our daily bread is the food we need, and it is the relationship we crave with God. St. Augustine of Hippo notes, "you have made us and drawn us to yourself, and our heart is unquiet until it rests in you."[11] We long to be fed by God, as a child is fed, or as a lover enjoys the company of her beloved. **This phrase of the Lord's Prayer is much more than a request for food. It is the desire of our heart reaching out to God.**

God responds by providing us with the essential food we need, and more. Our loving God also offers us relationship beyond our faint desires. God pours bounty on us, so that we can rest and not continue to strive for the *food that perishes, but for food the endures to eternal life, which the Son of Man will give you* (John 6:27).

And part of that food is the Bread and Wine that form the Lord's Supper, our Communion, our Eucharist. When we come to God in the celebration of the Eucharist, we are given the Bread that indeed "endures to eternal life." In receiving the communion bread, we are made "One Body with Him that He may dwell in us and we in Him," as Eucharistic Prayer I from the *Book of Common Prayer* says.

---

[11] https://www.piercedhearts.org/theology_heart/teaching_saints/ hearts_restless_st_augustine.htm

The Lord's Prayer: Walk in Love

Praying for our daily bread is much more than a request for food. **It is, if we allow it to be, an offering of ourselves to sit with God as our beloved and be filled with the simplest of joys and love.** In our fast-food oriented society, food can be about grabbing a bite on the go and getting on to the next thing. The same thing can be true in our relationship with God. We show up on Sunday, when it fits our schedule; but too often our minds aren't focused on worship. I sometimes (too often) catch myself making plans for the week, or fretting about the length of the sermon, or being distracted by the actions of a choir member. On those occasions when I really think about the worship of God, I am enriched, inspired, and find rest in God's presence.

WE SEE THE *WAY OF LOVE* IN THE LORD'S PRAYER

It can be difficult to take time to rest with God. There is so much going on in our lives. We are striving to get ahead, or just to keep the status quo. We think we *must* do this or that ministry because it is so important. Even though there are only 24 hours in a day, too often we fill them with 26 hours of work and entertainment and rushing around.

We forget that we need to be fed before we can give of ourselves in a meaningful way and not be burned out. Part of being fed is to rest our souls and bodies.

The *Way of Love* says, "It is necessary to Rest in God and let the lessons sink in, and Trust that God will provide. [We need to] receive the gift of God's grace, peace, and restoration. From the beginning of creation, God has established the sacred pattern of going and returning, labor and rest. Especially today, God invites us to dedicate time for restoration and wholeness—within our bodies, minds, and souls, and within our communities and institutions. By resting we place our trust in God, the primary actor who brings all things to their fullness."[12]

Praying for "our daily bread" and seeing it as an invitation to sit and rest with God may feel foreign at first. What has eating got to do with faith and spirituality? It is partly about awareness. Being aware of eating; and being aware of God. Sometimes, I sit down to eat and when I get up I couldn't tell you if the meal was good or not, or even what I ate. That's because my mind was elsewhere. I was listening to the news, or reading an article, but not paying attention to my food.

The same thing can happen when we don't take time to be aware that we need to rest in and with God. We may pray, but we do not feel refreshed, or even act as if we have time with God. Our minds are not pausing long enough in our planning and worrying to be aware that we are in the presence of our Creator, our Lover, our Friend.

Times of rest and restoration are essential. Too often, though, we push them to the end of our to-do lists. "I go to church." "I read scripture for five minutes every morning." "I do a retreat once a year." The list goes on and on as we excuse ourselves from really taking daily time to be with God as Lover and Beloved. We allow our time to get filled up with TV and Facebook. Sometimes it is necessary to make an appointment with God, or even physically put it on your calendar: "Meet God for a loaf of bread and jug of wine."

I am an expert at procrastinating and excusing my inability to take a retreat day, or two. If you are having trouble setting an

---

[12] https://www.episcopalchurch.org/way-of-love/practice/rest
46

appointment with God, ask yourself these questions. What am I afraid of encountering in the quiet with God? Why do I need to always be doing something? Would the world fall apart if I allowed myself time with God? **Take time to be aware of resting in and with God, who calls each of us "Beloved."**

WE READ SCRIPTURE

When we read the Bible, we discover that God is often calling people to times of rest, that is, to being present with God. **God promises that we won't lack anything if we do take time, like a Lover and Beloved, sharing a loaf of bread and a jug of wine.**

Praying for our daily bread may remind us of the gift of daily manna during the Exodus. In Exodus 16 we read *the Lord said to Moses, "I am going to rain bread from heaven for you, and each day the people shall go out and gather enough for that day* (Exodus 16:4). It was exactly enough for one day, and those who tried to hoard the manna discovered that it *bred worms and became foul* (Exodus 16:20).

God provided what the people needed. It was enough for each day, not extra to store and create a safety net against future lack. God promised to give the manna each day. All the people needed to do was to trust that God would be faithful.

Our loving God continues to supply our needs. Jesus tells his disciples, *it was not Moses who gave you the bread from heaven, but it is my Father who gives you the true bread from heaven. For the bread of God is that which comes down from heaven and gives life to the world...I am the bread of life. Whoever comes to me will never be hungry, and whoever believes in me will never be thirsty* (John 6:32-35). **We can trust that God will provide what we need!** The Eucharist itself reminds us that we are fed by taking time to be with Jesus.

The story of the two sisters, Mary and Martha, in the Gospel of Luke, can be a warning to us that it isn't necessary to always be busy and try to make everything perfect. Simplicity can be a virtue.

> *[Jesus] entered a certain village, where a woman named Martha welcomed him into her home. She had a sister named Mary, who sat at the Lord's feet and listened to what he was saying. But Martha was distracted by her many tasks; so, she came to him and asked, "Lord, do you not care that my sister has left me to do all the work by myself? Tell her then to help me." But the Lord answered her, "Martha, Martha, you are worried and distracted by many things; there is need of only one thing. Mary has chosen the better part, which will not be taken away from her." (Luke 10:38-42)*

Many of us can relate to Martha. We are always on the go, working to make sure everything is just right in our ministry and in our lives. It's not that it is bad to be a worker. It is about finding balance and taking time to sit at Jesus' feet sometimes. Mary knew that sitting with Jesus was feeding her on a different level from the food her sister was busy fixing. Martha, like so many of us, had to be reminded gently that an elaborate feast isn't always necessary.

Our daily bread of physical and spiritual sustenance is only possible when we pause to rest in and with God. Hymn 690 in the Episcopal Church *1980 Hymnal* is *Guide Me O Thou Great Jehovah*. It brings several images together. We are pilgrims needing bread and just like the Hebrew people were led by the pillar, we are strengthened and supported by our God. **When we depend on**

God, we will be filled and "want no more." Our singing is a form of prayer.

Guide me, O thou great Redeemer, Pilgrim through this barren land...Bread of heaven, Feed me till I want no more.

We are promised the Bread of heaven even before we ask. God is already pouring blessings upon us. We may forget or become distracted by the busyness that surrounds us and calls for our attention. Taking time to rest could give us a new appreciation for what we really need in life. And maybe it's not the next new gadget or dress. **Maybe it *IS* time to still our soul so we can be grateful for the daily bread.**

Resting with God refreshes us for doing the Kingdom work of love and justice exactly where we are right now. Resting in God's love and ability to provide eases our stress about what we need to get done. As Julian of Norwich said, "All will be well, and all manner of things shall be well." What it takes is time to rest and be fed physically and spiritually.

WE APPLY THE LORD'S PRAYER TO OUR LIFE

- ❖ How much "daily bread" do I really need?
- ❖ Omar Khayyam's poem says, "A loaf of bread, a jug of wine, and thou" are really all we need. Take time to sit with God who calls you "beloved" and imagine sharing a loaf of bread and jug of wine.
- ❖ We each need time to Rest with God. If you think adding an appointment to your calendar would help you to remember to fit God in, then do it.
- ❖ In what way(s) do you feed on the "bread of heaven"?

WE PAUSE TO CONNECT WITH GOD

Write your own prayer; or use this prayer to gather your thoughts about the ways our daily bread is a feast and a rest with God. You may want to include an offer to make an appointment with God.

Dearest loving God, I sometimes pray for daily bread as a demand for the food and material things I think I need. Make me more aware of the depth of your love in giving me more than physical bread, but also rest and refreshment in the form of your loving relationship with me. Amen.

The Lord's Prayer: Walk in Love

FORGIVE US OUR TRESPASSES AS WE FORGIVE THOSE WHO TRESPASS AGAINST US

The Lord's Prayer is one of the best-known prayers in the world. Because it is so well known, we run the risk of repeating it by rote and not listening to or thinking about what we are saying. I know sometimes I come to the end of the prayer, only to realize that my mind wasn't fully engaged, and my heart was somewhere else entirely.

The Lord's Prayer invites us into a time of recognizing God as Father and as the Creator of heavens and instigator of a new Kingdom. We are part of that Kingdom, called by our baptism to live differently so that we can indeed be part of bringing the new Kingdom to earth. So far, we have looked at four of the *Way of Love* disciplines which can help us live a fuller life. We've prayerfully looked at some of the ways that we pray, bless, learn and rest intersect with the Lord's Prayer.

Really living into the words of the Lord's Prayer would be life-changing if we took it seriously. The phrase right in the middle of the prayer is especially challenging. Jesus tells us to pray that God will "forgive us our trespasses, as we forgive those who trespass against us." We are called to turn and offer our mistakes, our failures, our misdeeds, our sins to our Father. Rather like a little child who knows she has done something wrong, we come bearing the brokenness of our lives and the brokenness we've caused to our Abba/Amma.

Many translations of the Lord's Prayer substitute the word "debts" for the word "trespasses." The connotation behind the two words changes the sense of the prayer just slightly, although both words imply being linked to someone else by our actions.

To "trespass" is to infringe on someone else's land, property, rights or to commit an offense against a person or rules. The word comes from the Old French *trespasser* meaning to pass over or across. The word debt, on the other hand, is based on the Latin *debitum;* which means something owed.

Whether we "trespass" by infringing on someone, or feel that we owe something to another, we are in a relationship with one another. **As we pray to be forgiven of trespasses, we are essentially recognizing that we have trampled on others in some fashion.** Perhaps we have ignored their boundaries or rights to being treated as equals. When we pray "forgive us our debts," we acknowledge that we owe everyone the right to be themselves and to be seen as a child of the Living God.

Some of the translations identify the trespasses or debts as actual "hurts." *The New Zealand Prayer Book* says, "In the hurts we absorb from one another, forgive us." The Times and Seasons.net translation pleads "may we reconcile with the people we've hurt, just as we reconcile with the people who've hurt us." Using the word "hurt" reminds us that we are either physically, or emotionally, harming another who, like us, is an image of God.

Realizing that we owe one another reconciliation and forgiveness, the Syrian Aramaic translation asks that we "loose the cords of mistakes binding us as we release the strands we hold of others' faults." This notes that we are bound together even when we sin against one another. It is only in letting go of the way(s) we have hurt or wronged others that we can be truly free. **It is in offering reconciliation (restoring relationship) that we free ourselves to move forward.** The word itself is rooted in the Latin *reconciliare*, meaning to bring back together.

54

The Lord's Prayer: Walk in Love

Turning to God, and asking for forgiveness for our trespasses, hurts, debts, infringements, or mis-uses of others makes us aware of our need to offer forgiveness to those who have hurt or trampled on us. We continue the prayer by saying, "as we forgive those who trespass against us."

Life is a two-way street. My actions and reactions have results. If I respond in irritation to someone who is inconsiderate of me, I compound the problem. I don't know why the other person is acting grumpy or being mean. In reacting from my own sense of entitlement, instead of from a place of understanding and empathy, a negative spiral continues. When I can be more forgiving, kind, and thoughtful, the dynamic of the situation may change. It may not; but my own soul will not be scarred when I can "release the strands of others' faults."

It is dangerous to our soul to harbor the resentments and coddle the hurts we perceive we have been subjected to by someone else. Science and medicine have determined that stress, including anger and resentment, have physical symptoms and can cause medical problems.

We need to remember that it is possible that the person you think "trespassed" did not mean anything personal by what was said or done. Maybe she had a fight with her spouse, or he has a bad headache. **Even if he did mean you harm, or abuse you, healing can only occur when we offer the injury to God.**

Sadly, we all know people who prefer to coddle their hurts. They refuse to consider that there might be a second side to the interaction. Sometimes, even the most even-tempered among us can hold a grudge. My mother was one of these. When she felt mis-used by someone, she could and did refuse to forgive that trespass. Her life gradually narrowed to a small circle of family and a couple of friends whom she trusted.

I often think how much richer her life could have been if she had been willing to "release the strands we hold of others' faults." There is a quote attributed to Buddha that says, "holding onto anger is like picking up a hot coal to throw at someone. You are the one that gets burned." By holding onto years and years of hurt, my mother harmed herself, and had no effect on the people she thought had sinned against her.

It is important to forgive and not hold onto our hurts and grudges, for they harm no one except ourselves. In the same way, we need to seek to reconcile and ask forgiveness of those we may have wronged, even if it was inadvertent. This is the reason victims of truly horrific events seek justice for the abuse they suffered even years earlier. In 1995 Nelson Mandela set up the Truth and Reconciliation Commission to help with that process in South Africa. He said, "We must therefore act together as a united people, for national reconciliation, for nation building, for the birth of a new world....Let freedom reign."[13]

N.T. Wright states that "the church is to be the advance guard of the great act of Forgiveness of Sins that God intends to accomplish for the entire cosmos...to pray [the Lord's Prayer] is therefore, in its largest meaning, to pray for the world."[14] **The healing of the soul is the heart of forgiving and being forgiven and leads to healing of the world.**

---

[13] https://www.azquotes.com/quote/658965
[14] Wright, *The Lord and His Prayer*, pg. 57

WE SEE THE *WAY OF LOVE* IN THE LORD'S PRAYER

Asking for forgiveness is about taking time to turn toward God or turn back to God. None of us is perfect; we all need to turn and ask forgiveness. The *Way of Love* explains it this way.

"Like the disciples, we are called by Jesus to follow the *Way of Love*. With God's help, we can turn from the powers of sin, hatred, fear, injustice, and oppression toward the way of truth, love, hope, justice, and freedom. In turning, we reorient our lives to Jesus Christ, falling in love again, again, and again."[15]

The "powers of sin" are the various things we need to ask for forgiveness about, because we all can slip into "hatred, fear, injustice, or oppression," often without meaning to or realizing that we are doing it. The slightest twist of your lip or roll of the eyes, when someone makes a mistake in pronunciation or uses the wrong contraction in a sentence, is the start of judging that person as "less than I."

The Letter to James warns against just that sort of subtle trespassing on someone's personhood. The author warns, *if a person with gold rings and in fine clothes comes into your assembly, and if a poor person in dirty clothes also comes in, and if you take notice of the one wearing the fine clothes and say, "Have a seat here, please," while to the one who is poor you say, "Stand there," or, "Sit at my feet," have you not made distinctions among yourselves, and become judges with evil thoughts?* (James 2:2-4) **By making judgements, we trespass ever so subtly on the rights of one another.**

---

[15] https://www.episcopalchurch.org/way-of-love/practice/turn

It is just a step or thought from judging someone inferior to us, to thinking that it is OK for women to be paid less, or migrants to be imprisoned, or poor children to have less well-equipped schools. Ben Franklin wrote, in *Poor Richard's Almanac*, "For the want of a nail the shoe was lost, For the want of a shoe the horse was lost, For the want of a horse the rider was lost, For the want of a rider the battle was lost, For the want of a battle the kingdom was lost, And all for the want of a horseshoe-nail." We might paraphrase that to recognize,

> For lack of love, insecurity was fostered;
> With lack of security, defensiveness was built;
> By lack of confidence, anger was fostered;
> Because of the anger, hurt was done;
> All for lack of love.

The Lord's Prayer and the *Way of Love* invite us to a different way. We are encouraged to live a "way of truth, love, hope, justice, and freedom. In turning, we reorient our lives to Jesus Christ, falling in love again, again, and again."

Forgiveness is a way of wiping the slate clean so we can once again see that God has written on it "You are my beloved child." The messiness of my life and yours, and of each person we encounter makes the slate dirty with erasures and corrections. Forgiveness rinses it off so the indelible Love shines through. We can fall in love again, again, and again.

In his book *The Butterfly Effect: How Your Life Matters*,[16] Andy Andrews states, "You have been created in order that you might make a difference. You have within you the power to change the

---

[16] https://www.andyandrews.com/ms/the-butterfly-effect/

world." Our actions as Christians, in being forgiven and forgiving others, can transform the world one circle of influence at a time. N.T. Wright exclaims, "As we learn what it is like to be forgiven, we begin to discover that it is possible, and indeed joyful, to forgive others."[17]

Recognizing that we have sinned or trespassed against someone else gives us the chance to make amends. Forgiving someone who has hurt us does not mean excusing the abuse. It means releasing the grip that the harm has on us. Even if we never hear "I'm sorry" from the perpetrator, we can forgive them. It unties us from being bound to the evil and hurt that happened. It opens the way for Love.

If my mother had been able to forgive those whom she believed had mistreated her, she would have been able to live a much fuller life. She would have looked for good, rather than feared and mistrusted people. Letting go of the injuries would have freed her to love and be loved.

WE READ SCRIPTURE

The Old and New Testaments both have a lot to say about forgiveness. Many times, in the Old Testament, God promises to forgive the ever-straying Israelites. Psalm 103 promises, *as far as the east is from the west, so far has he removed our transgressions from us.* (Psalm 103:12) If you think about it, the distance of east to west is infinite. Looking in any direction, when you have no obstructions, as on the top of a mountain, you can see for miles and miles and almost beyond the horizon. **That infinitely tiny speck beyond our vision is where God has put our iniquities.**

---

[17] Wright, *The Lord and His Prayer*, pg. 63

In the Book of Micah God is extolled as *pardoning iniquity and passing over the transgression of the remnant…[God] does not retain his anger forever, because he delights in showing clemency. He will again have compassion upon us; he will tread our iniquities under foot. You will cast all our sins into the depths of the sea* (Micah 7:18-19).

We now know a lot more than Micah did about how deep the oceans are. The average depth is 2.3 miles, while the Challenger Deep area of the Mariana Trench near Guam is nearly seven miles deep! If our sins are that far down, there is no way we can retrieve them!

We pray the Lord's Prayer asking, "forgive us our sins," and we can be assured that they are already erased, removed, thrown "into the depths of the sea." How can we respond to such grace and love? By "forgiving those who trespass against us."

Jesus addresses this in the Gospels and tells us that we must forgive. His own example of forgiving happens in the depths of his agony on the cross when he prays, *Father, forgive them, for they do not know what they are doing* (Luke 23:34). He is praying directly for the Roman soldiers in charge of the execution, as well as for the leadership that condemned him. He is also, of course, praying for us indirectly, as inheritors of the sins that separate us from one another and from God.

Earlier, his disciples ask him about who should be forgiven. In the Gospel of Matthew, *Peter came and said to him, "Lord, if another member of the church sins against me, how often should I forgive? As many as seven times?" Jesus said to him, "Not seven times, but I tell you, seventy-seven times"* (Matthew 18:21-22, and Luke 17:4).

A lot has been made of what Jesus meant by seventy-seven times, or as some translations say, seventy times seven. The actual number to calculate isn't the point. **We are not supposed to keep a score board of how many times we have forgiven someone.** We are simply to keep forgiving.

Jesus then goes on to tell the Parable of the Unforgiving Servant to stress how important it is to forgive one another. The parable tells of *a king who wished to settle accounts with his slaves. When he began the reckoning, one who owed him ten thousand talents was brought to him...out of pity for him, the lord of that slave released him and forgave him the debt.* The servant doesn't take his good fortune to heart, though and *as he went out, came upon one of his fellow-slaves who owed him a hundred denarii; and seizing him by the throat, he said, "Pay what you owe."* Even when the other man begs, he doesn't relent. When the other slaves *went and reported to their lord all that had taken place...his lord summoned him and said to him, "You wicked slave! I forgave you all that debt because you pleaded with me. Should you not have had mercy on your fellow-slave, as I had mercy on you?"...So my heavenly Father will also do to every one of you, if you do not forgive your brother or sister from your heart* (Matthew 18:23-35).

That seems like a pretty stern lesson. When we don't forgive, we are subject to worse punishment than the one who wronged us. In his Sermon on the Mount, Jesus takes it a step further. We ought to forgive and not retaliate even in the very act of being sinned against.

I say to you, do not resist an evildoer. But if anyone strikes you on the right cheek, turn the other also; and if anyone wants to sue you and take your coat, give your cloak as well; and if anyone forces you to go one mile, go also the second mile...Love your enemies and pray for those who persecute you, so that you may be children of your Father in heaven; for he makes his sun rise on the evil and on the good, and sends rain on the righteous and on the unrighteous (Matthew 5:38-45).

It is hard enough to forgive when we have been wronged. How much more difficult is it to forgive when someone is beating us or demanding our clothing? But that is exactly what we are to do. The Gospel goes even further than that. Jesus tells us not to harbor resentments in our heart when we approach God. He says, *whenever you stand praying, forgive, if you have anything against anyone; so that your Father in heaven may also forgive you your trespasses* (Mark 11:25).

God wants us to turn, as the *Way of Love* says, from the "powers of sin, hatred, fear, injustice, and oppression toward the way of truth, love, hope, justice, and freedom." However, until we forgive those who we think have hurt us, the slate is never fully washed clean. Our habit of harboring resentment will keep it dirty. **We can only be fully in relationship with God, when we are in true relationship with one another.** When we forgive those made in the image of God, we will be forgiven by God.

The Lord's Prayer: Walk in Love

WE APPLY THE LORD'S PRAYER TO OUR LIFE

- ❖ Which word: trespasses, debts, or hurts helps you see most clearly the harm our actions do to each other? Is there another word that encapsulates this even better for you?
- ❖ Are there ways you recognize that you judge others without really admitting that it is judgement? *eyebrows*
- ❖ In what ways, or times, do you find it difficult to forgive?
- ❖ Get a piece of chalkboard and paint "You are my Beloved Child" across it. No matter what else you may write on the chalkboard with chalk, underneath is the reminder that you are God's Beloved.

WE PAUSE TO CONNECT WITH GOD

Write your own prayer; or use this prayer to gather your thoughts about forgiving others and yourself as you turn to God. You may want to thank God for removing your sins so far away and ask for help in doing the same for others.

Forgiving God, too often I refuse to forgive those in my life who hurt me. I know that you freely offer forgiveness and my heart's actions block that. Help me to forgive fully, even to seventy times seven, so that you can fully forgive me, and I may more completely live into your truth, love, hope, justice, and freedom. Amen.

LEAD US NOT INTO TEMPTATION, BUT DELIVER US FROM EVIL

The Lord's Prayer is a core prayer for most Christians, not just because it is the prayer that Jesus taught his disciples, but because it encompasses all our basic needs, desires, and even fears. The prayer helps us recognize God's sovereignty and glory as well as our work in bringing the Kingdom of God to fruition. Through this prayer we ask God for what we need and are reminded that we too often trample on one another; and are trampled on. Paradoxically, we need to offer reconciliation, not anger.

Now we address how God helps us face our fears. We pray "lead us not into temptation but deliver us from evil." Every one of us has things we are afraid of, that could cause us to stumble in our faith walk, or that we don't even dare name. As the ancient prayer notes we want protection "from ghoulies and ghosties, and long-legged beasties, and things that go bump in the night." Those unnamed "things that go bump in the night" can be the most terrifying of all and we look to God for protection.

The New Zealand Prayer Book translation helps us to consider exactly how we want God to sustain us. "In times of temptation and test, strengthen us. From trials too great to endure, spare us. From the grip of evil, free us." **We plead for strength and freedom from things too hard to endure, trusting in the One who can protect us.**

Every day we are tempted by the world around us, and by our own thoughts and desires. We can be tempted to follow the crowd, even if it gets us in trouble. When I was in about third grade, a group of us were playing on a porch that was probably

66

four or five feet off the ground. It had a tempting concrete wall to jump from.

Everyone else was jumping off the porch and landing safely on the ground. I decided to join the fun. As I jumped, I realized I'd be in trouble with my parents for jumping off the high porch. I grabbed the porch pillar, which spun me back into the concrete instead of a safe landing on the ground. I smashed my foot into the concrete and broke several of the small bones in it. I got into more trouble that way; and learned a valuable lesson about following the crowd! I also spent the last month of third grade doing schoolwork at home. The elementary school had stairs and wasn't equipped for anyone on crutches (this was before mandated ADA improvements). Maybe I learned a lesson of compassion for those with handicaps during that experience, too.

We are also assaulted by dangers beyond our control; and threatened by the real evil in the world. *The New Zealand Prayer Book* affirms that we are speaking to the One who can strengthen, spare, and free us from any and all these dangers and evils. We have nothing to fear because we are looking to our Creator and Redeemer for help.

N.T. Wright says "Jesus victory over evil is also real and powerful...To pray 'deliver us from evil'...is to inhale the victory of the cross, and thereby to hold the line for another moment, another hour, another day, against the forces of destruction within ourselves and the world."[18]

The Lord's Prayer helps us get our priorities straight. When we are faced with the temptation to buy a new dress or give to a good cause, we ask God to strengthen us to make the right

---

[18] Wright, *The Lord and His Prayer*, pg. 72

choice. Sometimes it's not that simple. The lines aren't always neatly drawn or colored in black and white. C.S. Lewis warns that temptation can be subtle. **What we think is good, if taken to extremes, can become a trap and even evil.**

> "The most dangerous thing you can do is to take any one impulse of your own nature and set it up as the thing you ought to follow at all costs. There is not one of them which will not make us into devils if we set it up as an absolute guide. You might think love of humanity in general was safe, but it is not. If you leave out justice you will find yourself breaking agreements and faking evidence in trials "for the sake of humanity," and become in the end a cruel and treacherous man."[19]

The New Zealand Prayer Book notes, we will be faced with trials and tribulations in our life. We ask God to spare us "from trials too great to endure," trusting that God will indeed be in any challenging situation we face. Romans 8:28 assures us, *God causes everything to work together for the good of those who love God and are called according to his purpose for them.*

It can be difficult to remember this assurance when we are facing a hard diagnosis for ourselves or a loved one, or when a natural disaster strikes, or we lose our job. However, when we get past the trauma and look back, we will always discover God's hand was there.

There is a Taoist story that illustrates how we don't always know what is good or bad until we look back:

---

[19] C. S. Lewis, *Mere Christianity,* (HarperCollins UK, 2009), p.22,

The Lord's Prayer: Walk in Love

When an old farmer's stallion wins a prize at a country show, his neighbor comes to congratulate him, but the old farmer says, "Who knows what is good and what is bad?"

The next day some thieves come and steal his valuable animal. His neighbor comes to commiserate with him, but the old man replies, "Who knows what is good and what is bad?"

A few days later the spirited stallion escapes from the thieves and joins a herd of wild mares, leading them back to the farm. The neighbor comes to share the farmer's joy, but the farmer says, "Who knows what is good and what is bad?"

The following day, while trying to break in one of the mares, the farmer's son is thrown and fractures his leg. The neighbor comes to share the farmer's sorrow, but the old man's attitude remains the same as before.

The following week the army passes by, forcibly conscripting soldiers for the war, but they do not take the farmer's son because he cannot walk. The neighbor thinks to himself, "Who knows what is good and what is bad?"

Just like the farmer's neighbor who looked at the visible results, **it can be difficult to identify the hand of God when you are in the middle of some seeming difficulty.** There was a time in my life when I wasn't sure "what is good and what is bad." I had lost my job, which it turned out had been a hidden idol. I coveted the title and recognition, even though it was simply Director of Religious Education. I thought losing the job was the worst possible thing to happen. I was certain that my calling was in teaching Sunday School. However, over the next few months, and years, God showed me that my belief was not true.

What I thought bad at first, led to the publication of my first book, and later speaking engagements, and further books. I would never have guessed all that God had in store when I lost that job. God took me from the temptation of believing I was a wonderful Christian educator and showed me that there was a lot more to do in the Kingdom. I still need to be reminded to trust that God is in control, no matter what the outward appearances are. I still have my days of thinking I should do it all on my own. Then God taps me on the shoulder and says, "not so fast, dear one."

The Lord's Prayer is one way to refocus our hearts toward God. It is the way we are reminded that we are not alone. **We are strengthened and encouraged by the One who loves us.** Author James Cymbala notes, "The devil is not terribly frightened of our human efforts and credentials. But he knows his kingdom will be damaged when we begin to lift up our hearts to God."[20]

There is evil in the world. You cannot watch the news without acknowledging that. The Lord's Prayer asks God to "deliver us from evil." *The New Zealand Prayer Book* once again, takes it a little deeper. "From the grip of evil, free us," we pray. There will always be evil. It is part of the fallen condition of our world. Martin Luther stated, "The world is a den of murderers, subject to the devil. If we desire to live on earth, we must be content to be guests in it, and to lie in an inn where the host is a rascal, whose house has over the door this sign or shield, 'For murder and lies.'"

Because we are God's beloved though, we don't need to be in the "grip of evil." Even though the "inn [has a] host who is a rascal," we are not subject to that leadership. Through the cross

---

[20] https://davidwilkersontoday.blogspot.com/2014/03/the-real-force-by-jim-cymbala.html

and Resurrection, the power of evil has been broken. Author Francis Frangipane notes, "Jesus defeated Satan...not by directly confronting the devil, but by fulfilling the destiny to which He had been called. The greatest battle that was ever won was accomplished by the apparent death of the victor, without even a word of rebuke to His adversary!"[21]

In the power of God's love, we are defended from temptations, trials, and evils of the "world, the flesh, and the devil." **The Lord's Prayer assures of us God's protection through temptation and evil, freeing us to do the work of love and giving birth to the Kingdom of God.** Freed from fear, we can go and live the *Way of Love.*

WE SEE THE *WAY OF LOVE* IN THE LORD'S PRAYER

The Lord's Prayer is a way of maintaining our connection with God through prayer. Empowered by God's love we can "go in peace to love and serve the Lord" as instructed in the *Book of Common Prayer.* Even if there are stumbling blocks or hurts we need to forgive, and things in our lives that may make us fearful, we are assured that God is greater than all of them. Evil and danger are a reality in the fallen world, but our God is greater.

J.B. McClure in the book *Anecdotes and Illustrations of D. L. Moody Related By Him In His Revival Work* (published in 1881) quotes Moody, "Satan puts straws across our path and magnifies it and makes us believe it is a mountain, but all the devil's mountains are mountains of smoke; when you come up to them they are not there." In other words, what we perceive as huge problems, are just smoke and mirrors when seen through the eyes of faith. As we understand that truth, we can look beyond our

---

[21] https://francisfrangipanemessages.blogspot.com/2013/11/the-stronghold-of-christs-likeness.html

fears and prejudices and live as the *Way of Love* calls us to do as we Go.

> "Cross boundaries, listen deeply and live like Jesus. As Jesus went to the highways and byways, he sends us beyond our circles and comfort, to witness to the love, justice, and truth of God with our lips and with our lives. We go to listen with humility and to join God in healing a hurting world. We go to become Beloved Community, a people reconciled in love with God and one another."[22]

When we meet our Father in the Lord's Prayer, we do become a "Beloved Community...reconciled in love with God and one another." **Fed, forgiven, and freed from fear, we are able to go and become Kingdom builders "on earth as in heaven."**

The *Way of Love* that happens when we take time to pray and bless strengthens our faith muscles. When we pause to learn and rest we are enabled to see more clearly the path we are on and that God is beside us. The ability to recognize when we must turn provides us the opportunity to then go in the power of God's spirit.

God is with us when we release our fears and just go. We are encouraged to emulate Joshua as he prepared to enter the Promised Land.

> *Be strong and courageous; for you shall put this people in possession of the land that I swore to their ancestors to give them…This book of the law shall not depart out of your mouth; you shall meditate on it day and night, so that you*

---

[22] https://www.episcopalchurch.org/way-of-love/practice/go

72

may be careful to act in accordance with all that is written in it. For then you shall make your way prosperous, and then you shall be successful. I hereby command you: Be strong and courageous; do not be frightened or dismayed, for the Lord your God is with you wherever you go (Joshua 1:6-9).

Like Joshua we are to live into God's kingdom. We are to *love the Lord your God with all your heart, all you soul, all your mind, and all your strength, and your neighbor as yourself* (Matthew 23:37). When we follow this Golden Rule, **God is faithful to be with us sharing the burden and protecting us. God will show us the way to go in order to manifest the Kingdom in our lives.**

WE READ SCRIPTURE

The *Way of Love* invites us to go out into the world and make a difference. The Lord's Prayer teaches us that God is faithful, no matter what deceptive appearances there may be. Scripture affirms the promise of God's never-failing love.

Psalm 37:25 states, *Once I was young, and now I am old. Yet I have never seen the godly abandoned or their children begging for bread*.

In his Letter to the Romans, Paul announces, *For ever since the world was created, people have seen the earth and sky. Through everything God made, they can clearly see his invisible qualities–his eternal power, and divine nature. So, they have no excuse for not knowing God* (Romans 1:20).

Both these citations point our hearts to the grace of God. We go forth knowing that the godly are not abandoned. Everyone, believer or not, can *see [God's] invisible qualities—his eternal power, and divine nature.*

Jesus tells his disciples, *with man this is impossible, but with God all things are possible* (Matthew 19:26). God can even get *a camel to go through the eye of a needle* (Matthew 19:24). Appearances can trick us into thinking we are in danger or that something is impossible. However, God is always with us. It is our calling to face down evil and temptations in the name of God.

At the end of his earthly ministry, just before his Ascension, Jesus commissions the disciples. He tells them, *Go therefore and make disciples of all nations, baptizing them in the name of the Father and of the Son and of the Holy Spirit, and teaching them to obey everything that I have commanded you* (Matthew 28:18-20). He leaves them, and us, with a wonderful promise, *remember, I am with you always, to the end of the age.*

With God's empowerment, there is nothing we cannot stand up to. There is no power that can harm us eternally.

We are not alone in our Kingdom work of love. We are protected by the Spirit of the Living God. At the Last Supper, Jesus prayed for all disciples in all times.

I am asking on their behalf....Holy Father, protect them in your name that you have given me, so that they may be one, as we are one....I am not asking you to take them out of the world, but I ask you to protect them from the evil one....As you have sent me into the world, so I have sent them into the world....I ask not only on behalf of these, but also on behalf of those who will believe in me through their word, that they may all be one....I in them and you in me, that they may become completely one, so that the world may know that you have sent me and have loved them even as you have loved me...I

*made your name known to them, and I will make it known, so
that the love with which you have loved me may be in them,
and I in them* (John 17:9-26).

Our Lord asks that all believers may be one in the love of God. A
couple of chapters earlier, Jesus promises to give us an Advocate,
*the Spirit of truth who comes from the Father, he will testify on my
behalf. You also are to testify because you have been with me
from the beginning* (John 15:26-27). **The Holy Spirit helps us to go
into the world, to speak the words of love and walk in the way
of truth.** St. Paul also encourages the early church in Rome with
the promise of the Spirit.

*For all who are led by the Spirit of God are children of
God...you have received a spirit of adoption. When we cry,
"Abba! Father!" it is that very Spirit bearing witness with our
spirit that we are children of God, and if children, then heirs,
heirs of God and joint heirs with Christ—if, in fact, we suffer
with him so that we may also be glorified with him* (Romans
8:14-17).

Paul says we have the Spirit of God within us to help us go and
love as we are loved. Even when we suffer, we are loved and held
by the One who loves us and who we call Father/Mother. Paul
himself was confronted by many trials, evils, and temptations to
take the easy route. This doesn't stop him. He affirms, *the
sufferings of this present time are not worth comparing with the
glory about to be revealed to us....For in hope we were saved...if
we hope for what we do not see, we wait for it with patience*
(Romans 8:18-25).

Paul ends this chapter with a paean of praise saying, *If God is
for us, who is against us? He who did not withhold his own
Son, but gave him up for all of us, will he not with him also*

give us everything else? Who will bring any charge against God's elect? It is God who justifies. Who is to condemn? It is Christ Jesus, who died, yes, who was raised, who is at the right hand of God, who indeed intercedes for us. Who will separate us from the love of Christ? Will hardship, or distress, or persecution, or famine, or nakedness, or peril, or sword?...No, in all these things we are more than conquerors through him who loved us. For I am convinced that neither death, nor life, nor angels, nor rulers, nor things present, nor things to come, nor powers, nor height, nor depth, nor anything else in all creation, will be able to separate us from the love of God in Christ Jesus our Lord (Romans 8:31-39).

God will indeed be with us to lead us through trials and temptations and deliver us from the evils of the world! Truly, with Paul and the early Christians we can announce, *we are more than conquerors through him who loved us!* (Romans 8:37)

Because God is working with and in us, we are fully able to go into the world and create a way for the Kingdom of God. In the Sermon on the Mount, Jesus tells those present how this happens. We are to l*ove your enemies, do good to those who hate you, bless those who curse you, pray for those who abuse you....Do to others as you would have them do to you...love your enemies, do good, and lend, expecting nothing in return. Your reward will be great, and you will be children of the Most High...for the measure you give will be the measure you get back* (Luke 6:27-38).

Really living these words, counter-cultural as they are, cannot help but to change not only ourselves, but also those with whom we come in contact. N.T. Wright warns, "**you can't pray [this prayer] from a safe distance.** You can only pray them when you are saying Yes to God's Kingdom coming to birth within you...we are called to live and pray at the place where the world is in pain, so that the hopes and fears, the joy and the pain of the whole world may become, by the Spirit and in our own experience, the hope and fear, the joy and pain of God."[23]

Through the Lord's Prayer we ask for help to forgive, to find strength, and to live so that "your will [will] be done on earth as in heaven." God is with us and God will not leave us. God will love us even if we sometimes slip into temptations or fear. God is the loving Father we address in the Lord's Prayer. God is fully and totally love. **Our response as the Beloved Community, as Kingdom people, is to hold the pain and fear of the world in and to God's love.**

---

[23] Wright, *The Lord and His Prayer*, pg. 75-76

WE APPLY THE LORD'S PRAYER TO OUR LIFE

- ❖ What are some of the frightening things that go bump in the night? Can you offer them to God?
- ❖ Fed, forgiven, and freed from fear, we are able to go and become Kingdom builders "on earth as in heaven." Which of these gifts is most important to your faith journey?
- ❖ We are promised, *the Lord your God is with you wherever you go.* How does this thought give you the impetus to go and live more fully into the life you have been gifted with?
- ❖ In which of the scripture citations do you hear a call to go? Read and re-read that citation. Look it up in another translation and read it aloud. What are you moved to do?

WE PAUSE TO CONNECT WITH GOD

Write your own prayer; or use this prayer to gather your thoughts about what it means to go into the world led by the love of God. You may want to list some specific trials or temptations that you need help with.

Holy and Loving God, there are many temptations in the world and sometimes evil seems to be winning. Help me to look instead to your promises of courage and strength so that I am not afraid. Open my heart and mind to remember that you are with me through whatever happens, help me to see that the things I think are good and those that I consider bad are held in your love and care for me. You will not let me slip from your hands. Amen.

The Lord's Prayer: Walk in Love

FOR YOURS IS THE KINGDOM, THE POWER, AND THE GLORY FOREVER AND EVER. AMEN

We have discovered many things in our study of the Lord's Prayer. We've seen how it is the basic prayer for all Christians, and that it is remembered long after other prayers have slipped from our minds. Throughout this study, we've looked at the ways the Lord's Prayer helps us live into the *Way of Love*. The *Way of Love* and the Lord's Prayer together help deepen the meaning of both the prayer and the disciplines of Pray, Bless, Learn, Rest, Turn, Go, and Worship.

We have come full circle as we reach the end of the prayer. We began by praying to "Our Father" that the Kingdom of heaven might come and now we acknowledge that "the Kingdom, the Power, and the Glory" are God's from the beginning and until forever. We close the prayer with a paean of worship saying, "Yours is the Kingdom, the Power, and the Glory forever and ever. Amen."

The New Zealand Prayer Book says, "For you reign in the glory of the power that is love, now and forever. Amen." This reminds us that the Kingdom and Power of God is simply Love. **God's rule is not imposed on us; it is a choice we make to respond in loving relationship**.

The paraphrase by Leslie Leland Fields says, "We ask you all this because you are the King and this holy kingdom is yours, Power and majesty and strength is yours Glory and honor and praise is yours. Forever and always, Amen." We are asking because God is the "king" and in charge of us and the entire kingdom. Our response is to offer honor and praise.

In the Syrian-Aramaic translation we pray, "To you belongs the ruling mind, the life that can act and do, the song that beautifies all: from age to age it renews. In faith, I will to be true."

The *Times and Seasons* translation states this truth a bit differently: "For wherever grace and community abide, there you are with us; we are not alone. Blessed be." **The kingdom of God is a song that is formed by God's grace and by human community working together in loving relationship that makes all things one.** Each of us is an active part in bringing that dream to fruition.

Mark Roberts of the Fuller DePree Center notes, "When we hear the word "kingdom," we tend to think of a place over which a king rules. But, in Aramaic, the primary language of Jesus, the word *malku* pointed not so much to the place of royal rule as to that rule itself...This means when Jesus said, "The *malku* of God has come near," he was pointing to the coming of God's authority and power. He was fulfilling the role of the messenger of Isaiah 52:7: *How beautiful on the mountains are the feet of those who bring good news, who proclaim peace, who bring good tidings, who proclaim salvation, who say to Zion, "Your God reigns!"*[24]

The kingdom of God, or the rule and sovereignty of God, which we are called to work toward is a place of grace and community. It is filled and empowered by the "power that is love," and the "song that beautifies all." The glory of God is what strengthens us to work toward that kingdom because we are not alone.

The Rev. Jean Campbell (Diocese of the Rio Grande) stated in a sermon, "When we pray Our Father, we acknowledge our

---

[24] https://mailchi.mp/depree.org/the-kingdom-of-god-has-come-near?e=e9e6d45443

82

relationship with God who is Father, but we also acknowledge that we are brothers and sisters to one another, united in our life together in and through Jesus Christ. The Lord's Prayer is both vertical, in our relationship with God; and horizontal, in our relationship with one another."[25]

When we pray the last phrase of the Lord's Prayer, we draw together all the other parts of the prayer, and our lives, into an offering to God. We acknowledge that God is our provider, and that God is the only One who can give us grace to forgive as we are forgiven. God will *keep me as the apple of your eye; hide me in the shadow of your wings* (Psalm 17:8) so that we can indeed proclaim, "the Kingdom, the Power, and the Glory are yours, now and forever."

When we pray the Lord's Prayer in the Daily Offices, it comes immediately after our affirmation of faith in the Creed. In the Eucharist, it is said following the Eucharistic Prayer. In both instances, we are linking our lives with the original disciples as we recite the prayer they were taught by Jesus. The Creed and Eucharistic Prayer both unite us with all believers throughout the ages in their words and symbolism. We then respond by joining with believers everywhere, of all denominations and ages. We become one with the "great cloud of witnesses" spoken of in Hebrews 12:1.

At the very end of the prayer, we say "Amen." This simple two-syllable word means "so be it," or "let it be so." Amen means we are affirming participation in the words we just prayed. N.T. Wright notes that **when we pray the Lord's Prayer, we are aligning ourselves with participation in God's Kingdom.**

---

[25] sermon preached at Cathedral of St. John, Albuquerque, NM, July 23, 2019

It is "a prayer of mission and commission...[in which] we submit our lives to God's alternative kingdom-vision." Wright says the prayer is "one of incarnation and empowerment...to invoke the power of the Spirit of Jesus...[and] it is a prayer of confidence and commitment...that rounds off and seals off all the others."[26]

In the recitation of the Lord's Prayer, and by saying "Amen," we are affirming our desire to work to bring the Kingdom of God to life in the current broken and hurting world in which we live. This desire can take many forms. It may be active participation in a cause that works for justice or peace. It can be living as a positive presence at your workplace. It could be giving money or supplies to help with disaster relief. It might be raising your children as men and women of faith. I am fortunate to have the blessing, which not all parents have, to see my children living out their faith and raising their children to believe.

WE SEE THE *WAY OF LOVE* IN THE LORD'S PRAYER

The Lord's Prayer is a part of nearly every worship service we use. It is also a prayer that can be said alone. Individuals and groups can use the Lord's Prayer. Always, it is worship. It is the prayer that brings us full circle and re-centers our lives onto the *Way of Love*.

The *Way of Love* says that worship is when we "gather in community weekly to thank, praise, and dwell with God...we gather with others before God. We hear the Good News of Jesus Christ, give thanks, confess, and offer the brokenness of the world to God. As we break bread, our eyes are opened to the presence of Christ. By the power of the Holy Spirit, we are

---

[26] Wright, *The Lord and His Prayer*, pg. 86-87

84

made one body, the body of Christ sent forth to live the *Way of Love.*"[27]

Worship reminds us that we are a community. Even when we are praying alone, we are never truly alone. Everywhere in the world, others are praying. The Lord's Prayer is said in every language in the world. **Every minute of each 24-hour day is filled with the words of this prayer.** If we could only hear the chorus of those words, we would realize that we are in concert with millions of other voices of prayer.

The words of the Lord's Prayer bring us together from our various distractions and cultures. The words unite us across Christian traditions and denominations. The prayer transcends differences and opinions. As we pray; we are reminded that we have only one "Father." **We are called to become one people, united in love, so that God's kingdom can come, and God's will be may done.**

Each of us is invited into the community of worship that is universal. The prayer calls us to know we are beloved by "our Father in heaven." The words encourage us with the possibilities of love in God's kingdom, founded on love and buttressed by forgiveness. We trust that our daily needs will be met, both physically, by bread, and spiritually, by protection from temptation and evil. In knowing that we are beloved and cared for, we are enabled to offer God's love, even to those we might find it difficult to love by ourselves.

The Lord's Prayer forms us into the everlasting community of faith—the Beloved Community—which is the kingdom of God. When we remember that God reigns "in the glory of the power

---

[27] https://www.episcopalchurch.org/way-of-love/practice/worship

that is love, now and forever" (*New Zealand Prayer Book*), our unified assent in "Amen" can have true power to effect change in our lives and beyond.

WE READ SCRIPTURE

The Lord's Prayer is ultimately a reminder that we are truly part of a community. There are many verses in the Bible that affirm that we are one body. Perhaps one of the better-known references is 1 Corinthians 12 which states, *just as the body is one and has many members, and all the members of the body, though many, are one body, so it is with Christ. For in the one Spirit we were all baptized into one body—Jews or Greeks, slaves or free— and we were all made to drink of one Spirit* (I Corinthians 12:12-13).

The words could be modernized to read *we were all baptized into one body—Republicans or Democrats, Episcopalians or Baptists, right-wing or left-wing, believers or atheists...* The list could go on and on. We would be reminded that we are diverse, yet each of us is individually loved by the Holy One of the universe who is "our Father/Mother/Creator."

> In the Letter to the Ephesians, Paul calls for unity when he says, *I therefore, the prisoner in the Lord, beg you to lead a life worthy of the calling to which you have been called, with all humility and gentleness, with patience, bearing with one another in love, making every effort to maintain the unity of the Spirit in the bond of peace. There is one body and one Spirit, just as you were called to the one hope of your calling, 5one Lord, one faith, one baptism, one God and Father of all, who is above all and through all and in all* (Ephesians 4:1-6).

Praying the Lord's Prayer intentionally helps us to be open to the one-ness of our life in the Body of Christ. Indeed, as Paul continues, *we must grow up in every way into him who is the head, into Christ, from whom the whole body, joined and knitted together by every ligament with which it is equipped, as each part is working properly, promotes the body's growth in building itself up in love* (Ephesians 4:15-16).

As one body, we can join our voices together in a great "Amen" of assent to becoming the kingdom of God active on earth here and now. We can join hands and hearts in order to be, as St. Teresa of Avila says, "the eyes with which He looks compassion on this world." She tells us "Yours are the feet with which He walks to do good. Yours are the hands, with which He blesses all the world. Yours are the hands, yours are the feet, yours are the eyes, you are His body."

Understanding that we are God's chosen and beloved children, who are in the world to be the kingdom, we can offer our assent with Isaiah. After Isaiah has a vision of the Lord "high and lifted up," God's asks, *Whom shall I send, and who will go for us?* Isaiah, and we, can respond *Here am I; send me*" (Isaiah 6:8). We can add our "Amen" to the seraphs and other heavenly beings who sing, *Holy, holy, holy, the Lord God the Almighty, who was and is and is to come* (Revelation 4:8).

It is not always easy to say "Amen" and "Here I am" to God. We think God may ask us to do something we are not prepared for. There have been many times in my life when I have taken a leap of faith and felt rather like Indiana Jones in *The Last Crusade*. The scene where he must step out of the cave into what looks like air is heart stopping. And then, his foot lands on a stone bridge that was previously invisible.

When our two daughters were toddlers, we packed up and moved to Colorado. Our intention was to work on my father-in-law's hog farm. The farm industry is a bit volatile and we soon found ourselves wondering where the next paycheck might come from. God provided—often just exactly enough to meet the bills. After three years, and the birth of a third daughter, the farm adventure failed. The family returned to Albuquerque.

The day I sent my first book off to a publisher, with just a note saying, "you don't know me, but I saw your name on our church bulletin board," was a lot like stepping off the cliff. God honored that trust with a contract and more books to write.

Each time I step out into the unknown I find God has already put a bridge there. It is still not necessarily easy to take the leap of faith, but I know I can trust the One who is my Abba, my Amma, the One who created me and calls me Beloved.

You can too!

The Lord's Prayer: Walk in Love

WE APPLY THE LORD'S PRAYER TO OUR LIFE

- ❖ Often, we recite familiar prayers, like the Lord's Prayer by rote and don't really think about it. The next time you say the prayer, try to think about the words so that your "amen" will be a true assent to what you have said.
- ❖ Does it make a difference when you think about all the other women and men who are praying the Lord's Prayer at all times of the day and night?
- ❖ Who would you include in the list of those who are part of the one body, with whom you might not agree? Fill in your own sentence: *"one body—Jews or Greeks, slaves or free…"*
- ❖ Do you question your ability to respond to God's call, or can you say confidently with Isaiah, "Here I am, send me"?

WE PAUSE TO CONNECT WITH GOD

Write your own prayer; or use this prayer to gather your thoughts about God's kingdom, power and glory from now and forever.

Holy and Living God, you are high and lifted up, yet you love each of us individually. Help us to respond with the "amen" of our worship and the offering of our lives to become your kingdom, your hands and feet to the world. Amen and Amen

ADDITIONAL EXERCISE

As you read through the alternative Lord's Prayer versions here, you may feel moved to create your own prayer paraphrase to reinforce what you have learned in this book. Look back through your responses to the questions and to the ideas that surprised you. How would you express the ideas and themes in the Lord's Prayer?

Use your own words to address your Father/Mother/Creator/Parent/Lover and share your self-offering. You can read mine after my bio.

The Lord's Prayer: Walk in Love

LORD'S PRAYER VERSIONS

TRADITIONAL LORD'S PRAYER

Our Father, who art in heaven,
hallowed be thy Name,
thy kingdom come, thy will be done,
on earth as it is in heaven.
Give us this day our daily bread.
And forgive us our trespasses,
as we forgive those who trespass against us.
And lead us not into temptation,
but deliver us from evil.
For thine is the kingdom, and the power, and the glory,
for ever and ever. Amen.

CONTEMPORARY LORD'S PRAYER

Our Father in heaven,
hallowed be your Name,
your kingdom come, your will be done,
on earth as in heaven.
Give us today our daily bread.
Forgive us our sins
as we forgive those who sin against us.
Save us from the time of trial,
and deliver us from evil.
For the kingdom, the power,
and the glory are yours,
now and for ever. Amen. [28]

---

[28] Episcopal *Book of Common Prayer* (BCP)

ALL SAINTS FULHAM

Eternal Spirit, Life-Giver, Pain-bearer, Love-maker,
Source of all that is and that shall be,
Father and Mother of us all,
Loving God, in whom is heaven:
the Hallowing of your Name echo through the universe.
The Way of your Justice be followed by the people of the world.
Your Heavenly Will be done by all created beings.
Your commonwealth of Peace and Freedom sustain our hope and
come on earth.
With the bread we need for today, feed us.
In the hurts we absorb from one another, forgive us.
In times of temptation and test, strengthen us.
From trials too sharp to endure, spare us.
From the grip of all that is evil, free us.
For you reign in the glory of the power that is love, now and
forever. Amen.[29]

NEW ZEALAND *BOOK OF COMMON PRAYER*

Gender neutral

Eternal Spirit, Earth-maker, Pain-bearer, Life-giver,
Source of all that is and that shall be, Father and Mother of us all,
Loving God, in whom is heaven,
The hallowing of your name echo through the universe!
Your heavenly will be done by all created beings!
Your commonwealth of peace and freedom sustain our hope and
come on earth.
With the bread we need for today, feed us.
In the hurts we absorb from one another, forgive us.

---

[29] https://re-worship.blogspot.com/2012/01/alternative-lords-prayer.html, (Pryor's Bank, Bishops Park, London)

94

In times of temptation and test, strengthen us.
From trials too great to endure, spare us.
From the grip of evil, free us.
For you reign in the glory of the power
that is love, now and forever. Amen.[30]

LESLIE LELAND FIELDS' LORD'S PRAYER

Our Father who art in heaven,
Glorious, honored, loved, hallowed be your name.
Reveal your kingdom among us, here, now in ocean, tree, bush, and sky.
Cause your every purpose to be fulfilled on earth, just as it is fulfilled so perfectly in heaven.
We acknowledge you, Father, as our generous Provider, so we ask, would you give us each day the food we need (but no more, no less, so we live by trust more than by food)?
And would you forgive us the creaturely wrongs we have done, the debts we owe, the ways we have hurt others
As we ourselves forgive and free those who have wronged and hurt us?
Please rescue us, deliver us when we face tribulations, temptations, when we are drawn away from you rather than close to you.
Please rescue us from the destroyer, that evil one.
We ask you all this because you are the King and this holy kingdom is yours,
Power and majesty and strength is yours.
Glory and honor and praise is yours.
Forever and always, Amen.[31]

---

[30] http://home.earthlink.net/~haywoodm/EFM-WriteLordsPrayer.html
[31] http://www.leslieleylandfields.com/

GALILEAN ARAMAIC

Abba,	Father,
Yithqadash sh'mak.	May thy name be holy.
Tethe malkuthak.	May thy kingdom come.
The'wey ra'uthak.	May thy will be done.
Pitthan d-çorak hav lan yomden.	Give us today our needed bread.
w-Shbuq lan hobenan.	And forgive us our debts / sins.
Hek'anan sh'baqin l-haibenan.	As we forgive our debtors.
w-La "ul lan l-nisyon.	And lead us not into temptation.
Amen.	Amen[32]

SYRIAN-ARAMAIC
(TRANSLATION BY NEIL DOUGLAS-KOTZ)

O Thou, the Breath, the Light of all,

Let this light create a heart-shine within, and Your Counsel rule till oneness guides all.

Grant what we need each day in bread and insight.

Loose the cords of mistakes binding us as we release the strands we hold of others' faults.

Don't let surface things delude us, but keep us from unripe acts.

To you belongs the ruling mind, the life that can act and do,

the song that beautifies all: from age to age it renews.

In faith, I will to be true. [33]

---

[32] http://aramaicnt.org/articles/the-lords-prayer-in-galilean-aramaic/

[33] http://home.earthlink.net/~haywoodm/EFM-WriteLordsPrayer.html

TIMES AND SEASONS

Breath of Life, in whom we live and move and have our being,
Your presence fills all of Creation.
May justice and mercy reign, in our lives and in our world.
Today may our bellies be full, Our hearts warm,
And our fellowship open.
May we reconcile with the people we've hurt,
Just as we reconcile with the people who've hurt us.
Lead us not into a time of trial, but deliver us from evil.
For wherever grace and community abide,
There you are with us.
We are not alone. Blessed be.[34]

---

[34] http://www.timesandseasons.net/2011/the-lords-prayer-an-alternate-version/

BIO

Cynthia Davis has written seven highly acclaimed Biblical fiction novels, a couple of children's stories, and two works of non-fiction. Her history of St. John's Cathedral in Albuquerque, NM (*From A Grain of Mustard Seed*) was a major part of the documentation for the process of registering the Cathedral on the National Historic register. Davis leads retreats and studies based on her books, blog topics, and scripture. Her weekly blog has explored a variety of topics over the past decade, including Spiritual Scrapbooking, seasonal studies, *lexio divino*, and other topics. (FootprintsFromTheBible.blogspot.com)

Since Advent 2018, Davis, has written three blog series focusing on the *Way of Love* and how it can be applied to our lives as seen in and through scripture. The *Way of Love* practices, and how they can be integrated in so many ways into our spiritual and secular lives, intrigue her as she continues to explore the depths of this idea.

Cynthia Davis was on staff of St. John's Cathedral, Albuquerque from 2000 until retiring in 2019. She currently serves as Coordinator of Women's Ministry for the Diocese of the Rio Grande, planning and implementing retreats and other events about three times annually. Davis has been active in The Order of the Daughters of the King® for most of her adult life, including as diocesan president from 2012-18.

Married for over 40 years, Davis and her husband enjoy nature, their three daughters, and eight grandchildren.

CYNTHIA'S PARAPHRASE OF THE LORD'S PRAYER

Abba, Daddy, you are above all and in all.

Holy is your Name, your Essence, your Being.

May your Kingdom, your dream of One Body in community with itself be built so that your loving way can be done in all creation.

We ask for what we need each day, our food, our rest, our communion with you,

And we ask you to forgive us when we fail to love as we are loved.

Help us to break the bonds of discord and dis-ease that separate us.

Let us follow your path, not our own, so that we are not tempted by the easy or the evil paths.

Truly you alone are Holy and yours is the way that leads to life.

Yours is the way of triumph and the way of loving joyfully, now and forever.

So be it. Amen and Amen.

OTHER WORKS BY CYNTHIA DAVIS

FICTION

It is I, Joseph	1-58943-004-2
Beloved Leah	1-58288-220-7
Miriam's Healing*	978-0-557-00943-5
Rahab's Redemption	1-58288-215-0
Naomi's Joy*	978-1-58288-257-4
My Abigail*	978-1-58288-269-7
Mary, My Love	978-0-9844723-0-7
A Sampler of Bible Beauty*	978-0-98447-232-1

CHILDREN

Lester's First Flight	978-0-9844723-1-4
Molly Moss, a Parable	

NON-FICTION

From a Grain of Mustard Seed	978-0-557-02763-7

*Study guide available for this book.

These books are available from Amazon.com and the author.

It is I, Joseph; Rahab's Redemption; and *Beloved Leah* are currently out of print but may be available, used, on Amazon.

SOME RETREAT TOPICS BY CYNTHIA DAVIS

Bible Beauty Spa or Tea Party and Study (based on *A Sampler of Bible Beauty*)

Rooted in the Tree of Life (based on the life of Naomi from the Book of Ruth and Jeremiah 17:8)

Walk with Jesus (An Interactive Journey through Holy Week)

Enter the Tabernacle (Based on the *Book of Exodus*)

Dancing in the Footsteps of Miriam (Based on *Miriam's Healing*)

A study of Saul, David, and Abigail (Based on *My Abigail* and 1 Samuel)

See more retreat options online:

CYNTHIA DAVIS ONLINE
www.CynthiaDavisAuthor.com
FootprintsFromTheBible.blogspot.com
Facebook at Cynthia Davis Author

Made in the USA
San Bernardino, CA
28 June 2020

74505435R00060